The Essential BOB DYLAN

Amsco Publications
New York/London/Paris/Sydney/Copenhagen/Madrid

Photography
front cover: David Gahr
back cover: Jerry Schatzberg
pages 2 and 4: Ken Regan
page 112: Daniel Kramer

Published 2001 by Amsco Publications
A Division of Music Sales Corporation, New York

Order No. AM 969573
US International Standard Book Number: 0.8256.1838.X
UK International Standard Book Number: 0.7119.8763.7

Exclusive Distributors:
Music Sales Corporation
257 Park Avenue South, New York, NY 10010 USA
Music Sales Limited
8/9 Frith Street, London W1D 3JB England
Music Sales Pty. Limited
120 Rothschild Street, Rosebery, Sydney, NSW 2018, Australia

Printed in the United States of America by
Vicks Lithograph and Printing Corporation

Blowin' in the Wind 5

Don't Think Twice, It's All Right 8

The Times They Are A-Changin' 12

It Ain't Me, Babe 17

Maggie's Farm 23

It's All Over Now, Baby Blue 26

Mr. Tambourine Man 14

Subterranean Homesick Blues 31

Like a Rolling Stone 34

Positively 4th Street 38

Just Like a Woman 40

Rainy Day Women #12 & 35 20

All Along the Watchtower 44

Quinn the Eskimo (The Mighty Quinn) 28

I'll Be Your Baby Tonight 48

Lay, Lady, Lay 51

If Not for You 56

I Shall Be Released 62

You Ain't Goin' Nowhere 68

Knockin' on Heaven's Door 70

Forever Young 65

Tangled Up in Blue 72

Shelter From the Storm 76

Hurricane 80

Gotta Serve Somebody 84

Jokerman 88

Silvio 92

Everything is Broken 98

Not Dark Yet 104

Things Have Changed 107

Blowin' In The Wind

Words and Music by Bob Dylan

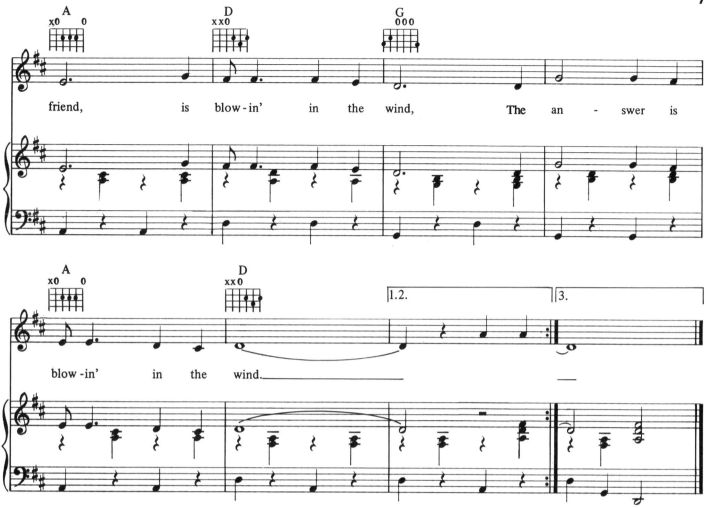

friend, is blow-in' in the wind, The an - swer is

blow-in' in the wind.

Additional Lyrics

3. How many years can a mountain exist
before it is washed to the sea?
Yes 'n' how many years can some people exist
before they're allowed to be free?
Yes 'n' how many times can a man turn his head
pretending that he just doesn't see?

The answer, my friend, is blowin' in the wind,
The answer is blowin' in the wind.

Don't Think Twice, It's All Right

Words and Music by Bob Dylan

The Times They Are A-Changin'

Words and Music by Bob Dylan

Additional lyrics

2. Come writers and critics who prophecize with your pen
And keep your eyes wide the chance won't come again
And don't speak too soon for the wheel's still in spin
And there's no tellin' who that it's namin'.
For the loser now will be later to win
For the times they are a-changin'.

4. Come mothers and fathers throughout the land
And don't criticize what you can't understand
Your sons and your daughters are beyond your command
Your old road is rapidly agin'.
Please get out of the new one if you can't lend your hand
For the times they are a-changin'.

3. Come senators, congressmen please heed the call
Don't stand in the doorway don't block the hall
For he that gets hurt will be he who has stalled
There's a battle outside and it's ragin'.
It'll soon shake your windows and rattle your walls
For the times they are a-changin'.

5. The line it is drawn the curse it is cast
The slow one now will later be fast
As the present now will later be past
The order is rapidly fadin'.
And the first one now will later be last
For the times they are a-changin'.

Mr. Tambourine Man
Words and Music by Bob Dylan

brand - ed on my feet. I have no one to meet and the

an - cient emp - ty street's too dead for dream in'. _____

Repeat three times

Refrain:

Verse 2. Take me on a trip upon your magic swirlin' ship
My senses have been stripped, my hands can't feel to grip
My toes too numb to step, wait only for my boot heels
To be wanderin'
I'm ready to go anywhere, I'm ready for to fade
Into my own parade, cast your dancin' spell my way
I promise to go under it.

Refrain:

Verse 3. Though you might hear laughin' spinnin' swingin' madly across the sun
It's not aimed at anyone, it's just escapin' on the run
And but for the sky there are no fences facin'
And if you hear vague traces of skippin' reels of rhyme
To your tambourine in time, it's just a ragged clown behind
I wouldn't pay it any mind, it's just a shadow you're
Seein' that he's chasin'.

Refrain:

Verse 4. Then take me disappearin' through the smoke rings of my mind
Down the foggy ruins of time, far past the frozen leaves
The haunted, frightened trees out to the windy beach
Far from the twisted reach of crazy sorrow
Yes, to dance beneath the diamond sky with one hand wavin' free
Silhouetted by the sea, circled by the circus sands
With all memory and fate driven deep beneath the waves
Let me forget about today until tomorrow.

Refrain:

It Ain't Me, Babe
Words and Music by Bob Dylan

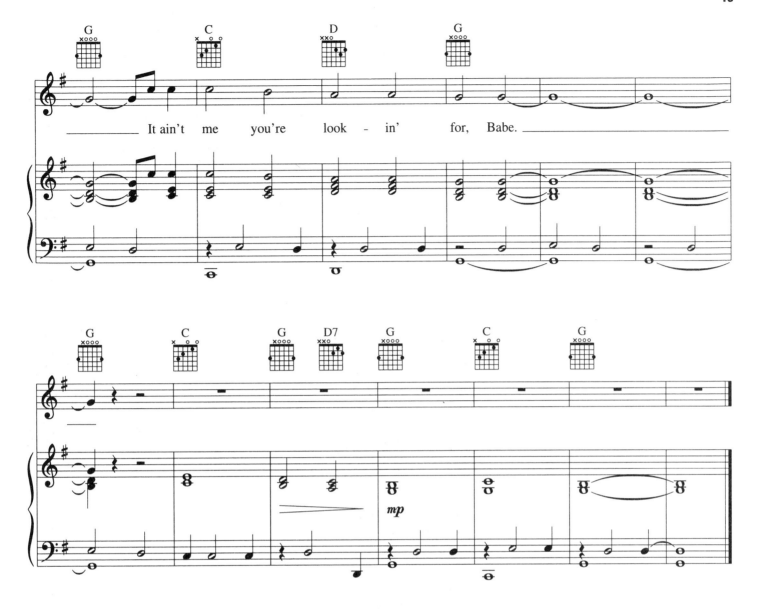

It ain't me you're look - in' for, Babe.

Additional lyrics

2. Go lightly from the ledge Babe,
   Go lightly on the ground,
   I'm not the one you want, Babe,
   I will only let you down.
   You say you're looking for someone
   Who will promise never to part,
   Someone to close his eyes for you
   Someone to close his heart.
   Someone who will die for you an' more
   But it ain't me, Babe,
   No, no, no it ain't me, Babe.
   It ain't me you're looking for, Babe.

3. Go melt back into the night Babe,
   Everything inside is made of stone,
   There's nothing in here moving
   An' anyway I'm not alone.
   You say you're looking for someone
   Who'll pick you up each time you fall,
   To gather flowers constantly
   An' to come each time you call.
   A lover for your life an' nothing more
   But it ain't me, Babe,
   No, no, no it ain't me, Babe.
   It ain't me you're looking for, Babe.

Rainy Day Women #12 & 35
Words and Music by Bob Dylan

Additional Lyrics

2. Well, they'll stone ya when you're walkin' 'long the street.
   They'll stone ya when you're tryin' to keep your seat.
   They'll stone ya when you're walkin' on the floor.
   They'll stone ya when you're walkin' to the door.
   But I would not feel so all alone,
   Everybody must get stoned.

3. They'll stone ya when you're at the breakfast table.
   They'll stone ya when you are young and able.
   They'll stone ya when you're tryin' to make a buck.
   They'll stone ya and then they'll say, "Good luck."
   Tell ya what, I would not feel so all alone,
   Everybody must get stoned.

4. Well, they'll stone you and say that it's the end.
   Then they'll stone you and then they'll come back again.
   They'll stone you when you're riding in your car.
   They'll stone you when you're playing your guitar.
   Yes, but I would not feel so all alone,
   Everybody must get stoned.

5. Well, they'll stone you when you walk all alone.
   They'll stone you when you are walking home.
   They'll stone you and then say you are brave.
   They'll stone you when you are set down in your grave.
   But I would not feel so all alone,
   Everybody must get stoned.

Maggie's Farm
Words and Music by Bob Dylan

Medium bright

1. I ain't gon - na work on MAG-GIE'S FARM no more ____

No, I ain't gon - na work on MAG-GIE'S

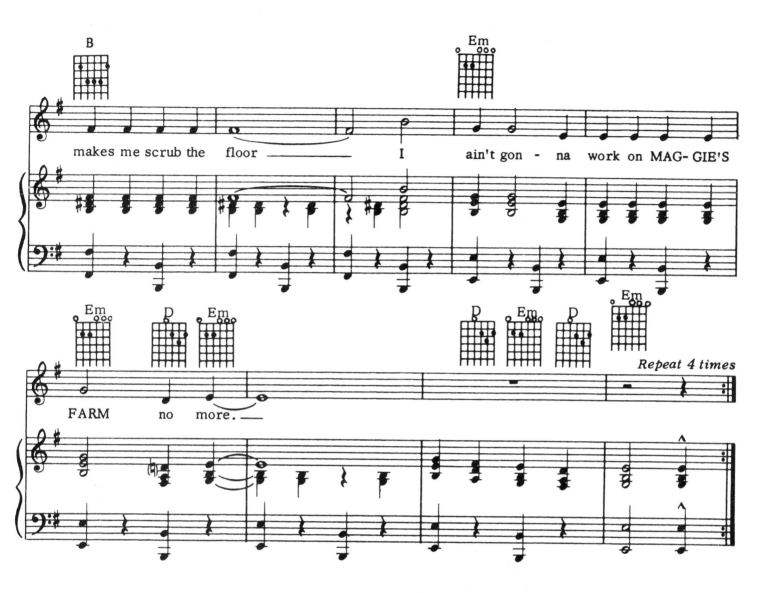

2. I ain't gonna work for Maggie's brother no more
   No, I ain't gonna work for Maggie's brother no more
   Well he hands you a nickel
   He hands you a dime
   He asks with a grin
   If you're havin' a good time
   Then he fines you every time you slam the door
   I ain't gonna work for Maggie's brother no more.

3. I ain't gonna work for Maggie's pa no more
   No, I ain't gonna work for Maggie's pa no more
   Well he puts his cigar
   Out in your face just for kicks
   His bedroom window
   It is made out of bricks
   The National Guard stands around his door
   Ah, I ain't gonna work for Maggie's pa no more.

4. I ain't gonna work for Maggie's ma no more
   No, I ain't gonna work for Maggie's ma no more
   Well she talks to all the servants
   About man and God and law
   Everybody says she's the brains behind pa
   She's sixty-eight, but she says she's twenty-four
   I ain't gonna work for Maggie's ma no more.

5. I ain't gonna work on Maggie's farm no more
   I ain't gonna work on Maggie's farm no more
   Well, I try my best
   To be just like I am
   But everybody wants you
   To be just like them
   They sing while you slave
   And I just get bored
   I ain't gonna work on Maggie's farm no more.

It's All Over Now, Baby Blue

Words and Music by Bob Dylan

2. The highway is for gamblers, better use your sins
Take what you have gathered from coincidence
The empty handed painter from your streets
Is drawing crazy patterns on your sheets
This sky too, is folding under you
And it's all over now, baby blue.

3. All your seasick sailors, they are rowing home
All your reindeer armies, are all going home
The lover who just walked out your door
Has taken all his blankets from the floor
The carpet too, is moving under you
And it's all over now, baby blue.

4. Leave your stepping stones behind, something calls for you
Forget the dead you've left, they will not follow you
The vagabond who's rapping at your door
Is standing in the clothes that you once wore
Strike another match, go start anew
And it's all over now, baby blue.

Quinn The Eskimo (The Mighty Quinn)

Words and Music by Bob Dylan

Additional Lyrics

2. I like to do just like the rest,
   I like my sugar sweet,
   But guarding fumes and making haste,
   It ain't my cup of meat.
   Ev'rybody's 'neath the trees feeding pigeons on a limb,
   But when Quinn, the eskimo gets here,
   All the pigeons gonna run to him.
   Chorus

3. A cat's meown, and a cow's moo,
   I can't recite them all.
   Just Tell me where it hurts yuh, honey,
   And I'll tell you who to call.
   Nobody can get no sleep, there's someone on ev'ryone's toes,
   But when the eskimo gets here,
   Ev'rybody's gonna want to doze.
   Chorus

Subterranean Homesick Blues

Words and Music by Bob Dylan

Moderate blues rock

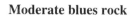

1. John - ny's in the base - ment mix - ing up the med - i - cine; I'm on the pave - ment

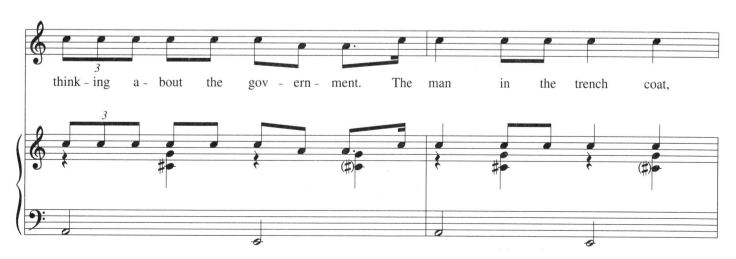

think - ing a - bout the gov - ern - ment. The man in the trench coat,

wants   e - lev - en   dol - lar   bills: You   on - ly   got   ten.

(after last verse, repeat intro and fade)

2. Maggie comes fleet foot
Face full of black soot
Talkin' at the heat put
Plants in the bed but
The phone's tapped any-way
Maggie says that many say
They must bust in early May
Orders from the D.A.
Look out kid
Don't matter what you did
Walk on your tip toes
Don't try "No Doz"
Better stay away from those
That carry around a fire hose
Keep a clean nose
Watch the plain clothes
You don't need a weather man
To know which way the wind blows.

3. Get sick, get well
Hang around a ink well
Ring bell, hard to tell
If anything is goin' to sell
Try hard, get barred
Get back, write braille
Get jailed, jump bail
Join the army, if you fail
Look out kid, you're gonna get hit
But users, cheaters
Six time losers
Hang around the theatres
Girl by the whirlpool
Lookin' for a new fool
Don't follow leaders
Watch the parkin' meters

4. Ah get born, keep warm
Short pants, romance, learn to dance
Get dressed, get blessed
Try to be a success
Please her, please him, buy gifts
Don't steal, don't lift
Twenty years of schoolin'
And they put you on the day shift
Look out kid they keep it all hid
Better jump down a manhole
Light yourself a candle, don't wear sandals
Try to avoid the scandals
Don't wanna be a bum
You better chew gum
The pump don't work
'Cause the vandals took the handles.

Like A Rolling Stone

Words and Music by Bob Dylan

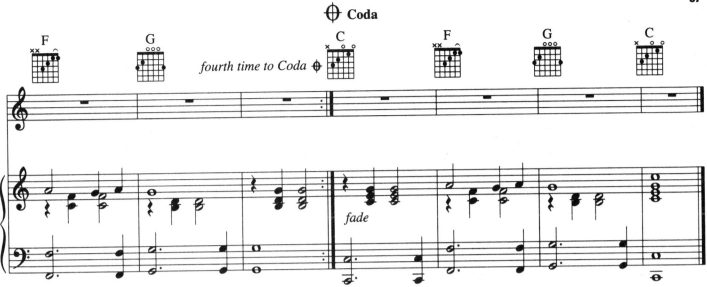

Additional lyrics

2. You've gone to the finest school all right Miss Lonely
   But you know you only used to get juiced in it
   And nobody's every taught you how to live on the street
   And now find out you're gonna have to get used to it
   You said you'd never compromise
   With the mystery tramp, but now you realize
   He's not selling any alibis
   As you stare into the vacuum of his eyes
   And ask him do you want to make a deal?
   Chorus

3. You never turned around to see the frowns on the jugglers and the clowns
   When they all come down and did tricks for you
   You never understood that it ain't no good
   You shouldn't let other people get your kicks for you
   You used to ride on the chrome horse with your diplomat
   Who carried on his shoulder a Siamese cat
   Ain't it hard when you discovered that
   He really wasn't where it's at
   After he took from you everything he could steal.
   Chorus

4. Princess on the steeple and all the pretty people
   They're drinkin', thinkin' that they got it made
   Exchanging all kinds of precious gifts and things
   But you'd better lift your diamond ring, you'd better pawn it babe
   You used to be so amused
   At Napoleon in rags and the language that he used
   Go to him now, he calls you, you can't refuse
   When you got nothing, you got nothing to lose
   You're invisible now, you got no secrets to conceal.
   Chorus

Positively 4th Street

Words and Music by Bob Dylan

2. You got a lotta nerve
    To say you gotta helping hand to lend
    You just want to be on
    The side that's winning

3. You say I let you down
    You know it's not like that
    If you're so hurt
    Why then don't you show it

4. You say you lost your faith
    But that's not where it's at
    You had no faith to lose
    And you know it

5. I know the reason
    That you talk behind my back
    I used to be among the crowd
    You're in with

6. Do you take me for such a fool
    To think I'd make contact
    With the one who tries to hide
    When he don't know to begin with

7. You see me on the street
    You always act surprised
    You say "how are you?", "good luck"
    But you don't mean it

8. When you know as well as me
    You'd rather see me paralyzed
    Why don't you just come out once
    And scream it

9. No I do not feel that good
    When I see the heart breaks you embrace
    If I was a master thief
    Perhaps I'd rob them

10. And now I know you're dissatisfied
    With your position and your place
    Don't you understand
    It's not my problem

11. I wish that for just one time
    You could stand inside my shoes
    And just for that one moment
    I could be you

12. Yes I wish that for just one time
    You could stand inside my shoes
    You'd know what a drag it is
    To see you

Just Like A Woman

Words and Music by Bob Dylan

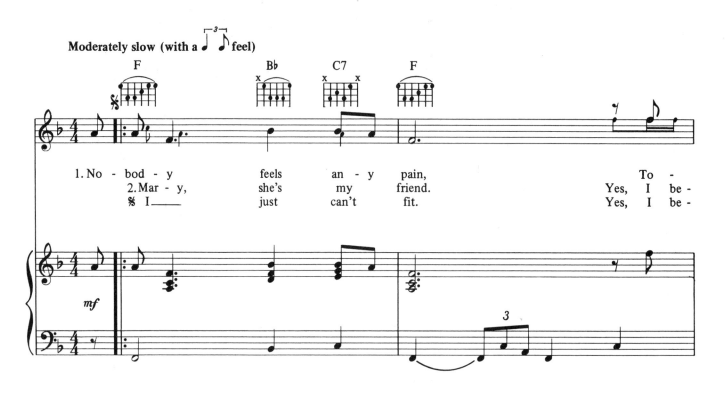

All Along The Watchtower

Words and Music by Bob Dylan

I'll Be Your Baby Tonight
Words and Music by Bob Dylan

Close your eyes,_____ Close the door,__
(Shut the) light,_____ Shut the shade,__

You don't have to wor - ry _____ an - y - more,_
You don't have _____ to be a - fraid,_

I'll_____ be your _____ ba - by to -

night. _____ Shut the

Well, that mock - ing - bird's gon - na sail _ a - way, _____

We're gon - na for - get it, That big, fat moon _ is gon - na

shine like a spoon, _ But, we're gon - na let it, You won't re - gret it. Kick your

shoes off,__ Do not fear,__ Bring that bot-

-tle o-ver here,__

I'll _____ be your _____ ba-by to-

night. _____

Lay, Lady, Lay

Words and Music by Bob Dylan

Slowly

If Not For You
Words and Music by Bob Dylan

I Shall Be Released

Words and Music by Bob Dylan

Additional Lyrics

2. Down here next to me in this lonely crowd
   Is a man who swears he's not to blame.
   All day long I hear him cry so loud,
   Calling out that he's been framed.

   Chorus

3. They say ev'rything can be replaced,
   Yet ev'ry distance is not near.
   So I remember ev'ry face
   Of ev'ry man who put me here.

   Chorus

Forever Young

Words and Music by Bob Dylan

Moderately slow, with a steady beat

You Ain't Goin' Nowhere

Words and Music by Bob Dylan

Knockin' On Heaven's Door

Words and Music by Bob Dylan

Tangled Up In Blue
Words and Music by Bob Dylan

Additional Lyrics

2. She was married when we first met,
   Soon to be divorced.
   I helped her out of a jam, I guess,
   But I used a little too much force.
   We drove that car as far as we could,
   Abandoned it out West.
   Split up on a dark sad night,
   Both agreeing it was best.
   She turned around to look at me,
   As I was walkin' away.
   I heard her say over my shoulder,
   "We'll meet again some day
   on the avenue."
   Tangled up in blue.

3. I had a job in the great north woods,
   Working as a cook for a spell.
   But I never did like it all that much,
   And one day the axe just fell.
   So I drifted down to New Orleans,
   Where I happened to be employed.
   Workin' for a while on a fishin' boat,
   Right outside of Delacroix.
   But all the while I was alone,
   The past was close behind.
   I seen a lot of women,
   But she never escaped my mind,
   And I just grew.
   Tangled up in blue.

4. She was workin' in a topless place,
   And I stopped in for a beer.
   I just kept lookin' at the side of her face,
   In the spotlight so clear.
   And later on as the crowd thinned out,
   I's just about to do the same.
   She was standing there in back of my chair,
   Said to me, "Don't I know your name?"
   I muttered somethin' underneath my breath,
   She studied the lines on my face.
   I must admit I felt a little uneasy,
   When she bent down to tie the laces
   Of my shoe.
   Tangled up in blue.

5. She lit a burner on the stove,
   And offered me a pipe.
   "I thought you'd never say hello," she said,
   "You look like the silent type."
   Then she opened up a book of poems,
   And handed it to me.
   Written by an Italian poet
   From the thirteenth century.
   And every one of them words rang true,
   And glowed like burnin' coal.
   Pourin' off of every page,
   Like it was written in my soul
   From me to you.
   Tangled up in blue.

6. I lived with them on Montague Street,
   In a basement down the stairs.
   There was music in the cafes at night,
   And revolution in the air.
   Then he started into dealing with slaves,
   And something inside of him died.
   She had to sell everything she owned,
   And froze up inside.
   And when finally the bottom fell out,
   I became withdrawn.
   The only thing I knew how to do,
   Was to keep on keepin' on,
   Like a bird that flew.
   Tangled up in blue.

7. So now I'm goin' back again,
   I got to get to her somehow.
   All the people we used to know,
   They're an illusion to me now.
   Some are mathematicians,
   Some are carpenters' wives.
   Don't know how it all got started,
   I don't know what they're doin' with their lives.
   But me, I'm still on the road,
   Headin' for another joint.
   We always did feel the same,
   We just saw it from a different point
   Of view.
   Tangled up in blue.

Shelter From the Storm

Words and Music by Bob Dylan

1. 'Twas in an-oth-er life-time, one of toil and blood,____
word was spoke be-tween__ us, there was lit-tle risk in-volved;
ly I turned a-round__ and she was stand-in' there____
dep-u-ty walks on hard__ nails and the preach-er rides a mount;____
lit-tle hill-top vil-age they gam-bled for my clothes;____

when black-ness was a vir-tue and the
ev-'ry-thing up to__ that point had been
with sil-ver brace-lets on__ her wrists and
but noth-ing real-ly mat-ters much, it's
I bar-gained for sal-va-tion an' they

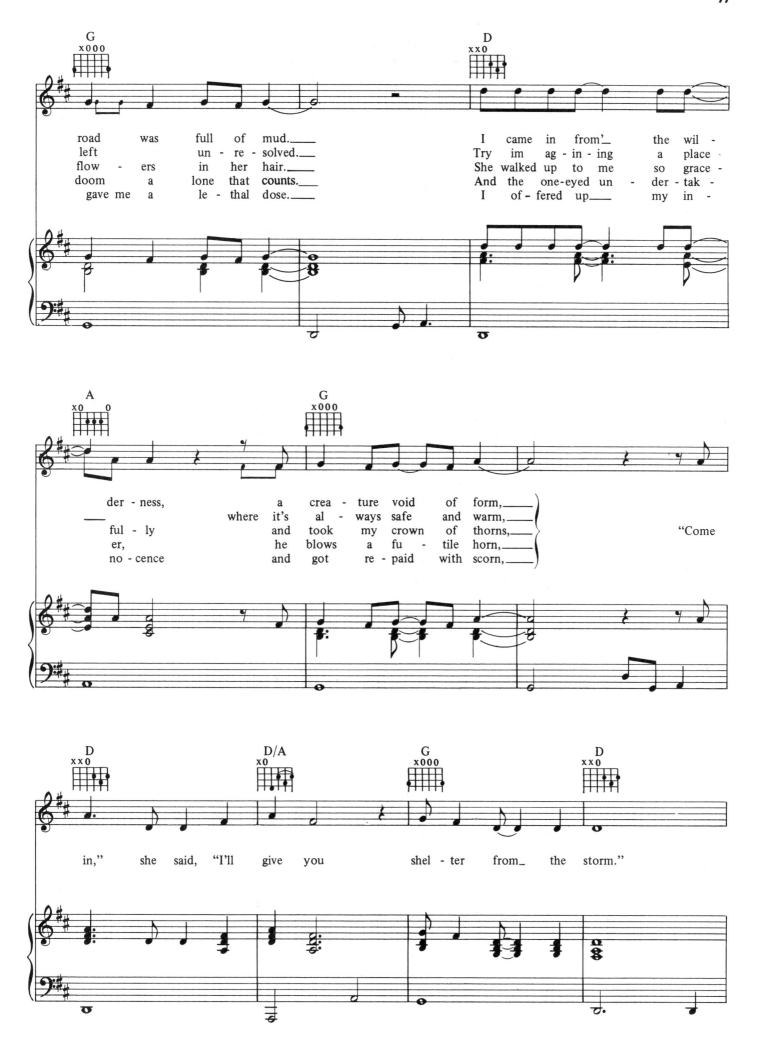

Hurricane
Words and Music by Bob Dylan and Jacques Levy

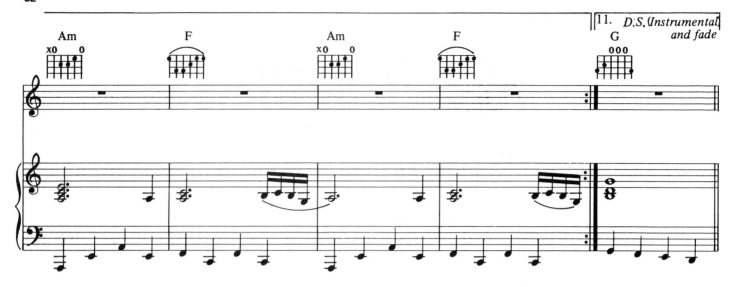

Additional Lyrics

2. Three bodies lyin' there does Patty see,
   And another man named Bello, movin' around mysteriously.
   "I didn't do it," he says, and he throws up his hands,
   "I was only robbin' the register, I hope you understand,
   I saw them leavin'," he says, and he stops.
   "One of us had better call up the cops."
   And so Patty calls the cops,
   And they arrive on the scene with their red lights flashin'
   In the hot New Jersey night.

3. Meanwhile, far away in another part of town,
   Rubin Carter and a couple of friends are drivin' around.
   Number one contender for the middleweight crown,
   Had no idea what kinda shit was about to go down,
   When a cop pulled him over to the side of the road,
   Just like the time before and the time before that.
   In Paterson that's just the way things go,
   If you're black you might as well not show up on the street,
   'Less you wanna draw the heat.

4. Alfred Bello had a partner and he had a rap for the cops,
   Him and Arthur Dexter Bradley were just out prowlin' around.
   He said, "I saw two men runnin' out, they looked like middleweights.
   They jumped into a white car with out-of-state plates."
   And Miss Patty Valentine just nodded her head,
   Cop said, "Wait a minute boys, this one's not dead."
   So they took him to the infirmary,
   And though this man could hardly see,
   They told him that he could identify the guilty men.

5. Four in the mornin' and they haul Rubin in,
   Take him to the hospital and they bring him upstairs.
   The wounded man looks up through his one dyin' eye,
   Says, "Wha'd you bring him in here for? He ain't the guy!"
   Yes, here's the story of the Hurricane,
   The man the authorities came to blame,
   For somethin' that he never done.
   Put in a prison cell, but one time he coulda been
   The champion of the world.

6. Four months later, the ghettos are in flame,
   Rubin's in South America, fightin' for his name,
   While Arthur Dexter Bradley's still in the robbery game,
   And the cops are puttin' the screws to him, lookin' for somebody to blame,
   "Remember that murder that happened in a bar?"
   "Remember you said you saw the getaway car?"
   "You think you'd like to play ball with the law?"
   "Think it mighta been that fighter that you saw runnin' that night?"
   "Don't forget that you are white."

7. Arthur Dexter Bradley said, "I'm really not sure,"
   Cops said, "A poor boy like you could use a break.
   We got you for the motel job and we're talkin' to your friend Bello,
   Now you don't wanna have to go back to jail, be a nice fellow.
   You'll be doin' society a favor,
   That sonofabitch is brave and gettin' braver.
   We want to put his ass in stir,
   We want to pin this triple murder on him,
   He ain't no Gentleman Jim."

8. Rubin could take a man out with just one punch,
   But he never did like to talk about it all that much.
   "It's my work," he'd say, "and I do it for pay.
   And when it's over I'd just as soon go on my way,
   Up to some paradise,
   Where the trout streams flow and the air is nice,
   And ride a horse along a trail."
   But then they took him to the jail house,
   Where they try to turn a man into a mouse.

9. All of Rubin's cards were marked in advance,
   The trial was a pig-circus, he never had a chance.
   The judge made Rubin's witnesses drunkards from the slums,
   To the white folks who watched he was a revolutionary bum.
   And to the black folks he was just a crazy nigger,
   No one doubted that he pulled the trigger,
   And though they could not produce the gun,
   The D. A. said he was the one who did the deed.
   And the all-white jury agreed.

10. Rubin Carter was falsely tried,
    The crime was murder-one, guess who testified?
    Bello and Bradley, and they both baldly lied,
    And the newspapers, they all went along for the ride.
    How can the life of such a man
    Be in the palm of some fool's hand?
    To see him obviously framed,
    Couldn't help but make me feel ashamed to live in a land
    Where justice is a game.

11. Now all the criminals in their coats and their ties
    Are free to drink martinis and watch the sun rise,
    While Rubin sits like Buddha in a ten-foot cell,
    An innocent man in a living hell.
    That's the story of the Hurricane,
    But it won't be over till they clear his name,
    And give him back the time he's done,
    Put in a prison cell, but one time he coulda been
    The champion of the world.

Gotta Serve Somebody
Words and Music by Bob Dylan

Additional Lyrics

2. You might be a rock'n'roll addict prancing on the stage.
   You might have drugs at your command, women in a cage.
   You may be a businessman or some high degree thief.
   They may call you doctor, or they may call you chief.
   Chorus

3. You may be a state trooper, you might be a young Turk.
   You might be the head of some big TV network.
   You may be rich or poor, you may be blind or lame.
   You may be leaving in another country under another name.
   Chorus

4. You may be a construction worker working on a home.
   You may be living in a mansion, or you might live in a dome.
   You might own guns and you might even own tanks.
   You might be somebody's landlord, you might even own banks.
   Chorus

5. You may be a preacher with your spiritual pride.
   You may be a city councilman taking bribes on the side.
   You may be workin' in a barbershop, you may know how to cut hair.
   You may be somebody's mistress, may be somebody's heir.
   Chorus

6. Might like to wear cotton, might like to wear silk.
   Might like to drink whiskey, might like to drink milk.
   You might like to eat caviar, you might like to eat bread.
   You may be sleeping on the floor, sleeping in a king-sized bed.
   Chorus

7. You may call me Terry, you may call me Timmy.
   You may call me Bobby, you may call me Zimmy.
   You may call me R.J., you may call me Ray.
   You may call me anything, but no matter what you say.
   Chorus

Jokerman
Words and Music by Bob Dylan

Additional Lyrics

2. So swiftly the sun sets in the sky.
   You rise up and say goodbye to no one.
   Fools rush in where angels fear to tread.
   Both of their futures, so full of dread, you don't show one.
   Shedding off one more layer of skin,
   Keeping one step ahead of the persecutor within.
   Chorus

3. You're a man of the mountains, you can walk on the clouds.
   Manipulator of crowds, you're a dream twister.
   You're going to Sodom and Gomorrah,
   But what do you care? Ain't nobody there would want to marry your sister.
   Friend to the martyr, a friend to the woman of shame,
   You look into the fiery furnace, see the rich man without any name.
   Chorus

4. Well, the Book of Leviticus and Deuteronomy,
   The law of the jungle and the sea are your only teachers.
   In the smoke of the twilight on a milk-white steed,
   Michelangelo indeed could've carved out your features.
   Resting in the fields, far from the turbulent space,
   Half asleep near the stars with a small dog licking your face.
   Chorus

5. Well, the rifleman's stalking the sick and the lame,
   Preacherman seeks the same, who'll get there first is uncertain.
   Nightsticks and water cannons, teargas, padlocks,
   Molotov cocktails and rocks behind every curtain.
   Falsehearted judges dying in the webs that they spin,
   Only a matter of time till night comes steppin' in.
   Chorus

6. It's a shadowy world, skies are slippery grey.
   A woman just gave birth to a prince today and dressed him in scarlet.
   He'll put the priest in his pocket, put the blade to the heat,
   Take the motherless children off the street,
   And place them at the feet of a harlot.
   Oh, Jokerman, you know what he wants,
   Oh, Jokerman, you don't show any response.
   Chorus

Silvio

Words and Music by Bob Dylan and Robert Hunter

Everything Is Broken
Words and Music by Bob Dylan

Moderately, with a steady beat

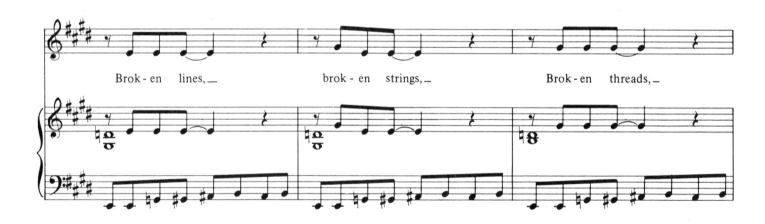

Not Dark Yet

Words and Music by Bob Dylan

Additional lyrics

2. Well my sense of humanity has gone down the drain
Behind every beautiful thing there's been some kind of pain
She wrote me a letter and she wrote it so kind
She put down in writing what was in her mind
I just don't see why I should even care
It's not dark yet, but it's getting there

3. Well, I've been to London and I've been to gay Paree
I've followed the river and I got to the sea
I've been down on the bottom of a world full of lies
I ain't looking for nothing in anyone's eyes
Sometimes my burden seems more than I can bear
It's not dark yet, but it's getting there

4. *Instrumental solo*

5. I was born here and I'll die here against my will
I know it looks like I'm moving, but I'm standing still
Every nerve in my body is so vacant and numb
I can't even remember what it was I came here to get away from
Don't even hear a murmur of a prayer
It's not dark yet, but it's getting there.

Things Have Changed

Words and Music by Bob Dylan

Additional lyrics:

2. This place ain't doing me any good
   I'm in the wrong town, I should be in Hollywood
   Just for a second there I thought I saw something move
   Gonna take dancing lessons do the jitterbug rag
   Ain't no shortcuts, gonna dress in drag
   Only a fool in here would think he's got anything to prove

   Lot of water under the bridge, Lot of other stuff too
   Don't get up gentlemen, I'm passing through

   People are crazy and times are strange
   I'm locked in tight, I'm out of range
   I used to care, but things have changed

3. I've been walking forty miles of bad road
   If the bible is right, the world will explode
   I've been trying to get as far away from myself as I can
   Some things are too hot to touch
   The human mind can only stand so much
   You can't win without losing a hand

   Feel like falling in love with the first woman I meet
   Putting her in a wheel barrow and wheeling her down the street

   People are crazy and times are strange
   I'm locked in tight, I'm out of range
   I used to care, but things have changed

4. I hurt easy, I just don't show it
   You can hurt someone and not even know it
   The next sixty seconds could be like an eternity
   Gonna get low down, gonna fly high
   All the truth in the world adds up to one big lie
   I'm in love with a woman who don't even appeal to me

   Mr. Jinx and Miss Lucy, they jumped in the lake
   I'm not that eager to make a mistake

   People are crazy and times are strange
   I'm locked in tight, I'm out of range
   I used to care, but things have changed